MW00989839

Beautiful Eucharist

Beautiful Eucharist

Published by Wellspring
An Imprint of Viident

ISBN: 978-1-63582-517-6 (hardcover)
ISBN: 978-1-63582-518-3 (eBook)

Designed by Ashley Dias

10 9 8 7 6 5 4 3

FIRST EDITION

Printed in the United States of America

"Encountering Jesus in the Eucharist
should be like touching Heaven,
and that should change the way
we live here on earth!"

— Matthew Kelly —

Table of Contents

INTRODUCTION: ASTONISHING
Matthew Kelly
1

1. MASS WAS BORING . . . UNTIL THIS HAPPENED
Jackie Francois Angel
11

2. WHY DO YOU DO THAT?
Father Mike Schmitz
17

3. DO YOU KNOW WHERE YOU'RE GOING?
Lisa M. Hendey
23

4. WHAT I LEARNED FROM A MUSLIM ABOUT THE EUCHARIST
Peter Kreeft
33

5. COME AWAY TO A QUIET PLACE
Jenna Greiwe
41

6. RIGHT HERE, RIGHT NOW, NO OTHER PLACE I'D RATHER BE!
Bishop Andrew Cozzens
47

7. YOUR MOST URGENT NEED
Fulton Sheen
53

8. THE EUCHARIST: GOD'S HIDING & OUR SEEKING
Bobby Angel
59

9. THE ULTIMATE PROOF OF GOD'S LOVE
Father Eric Boelscher
67

10. THIRTY WORDS THAT REVOLUTIONIZED MY LIFE
Dr. Allen Hunt
75

11. WHY I LIED TO MY PASTOR ABOUT FIRST COMMUNION
Sister Helena Burns, FSP
83

12. WHY DIDN'T ANYONE TELL ME THIS?
Matt Warner
91

CONCLUSION: GET CLOSE AND STAY CLOSE
Matthew Kelly
99

INTRODUCTION: ASTONISHING

— Matthew Kelly —

For most of Jesus' public life people crowded around him. If he was teaching in the synagogue, they crowded around him. If he was walking in the street, they crowded around him. If he was having a meal in a home, they crowded around him.

But there were two times when people fled from Jesus.

The obvious one was after his arrest and crucifixion. Where were all the crowds that had followed him? Where were all those people who witnessed his miracles? Where were all the people he had cured and fed? Where were the crowds of people who cheered him into the city less than a week ago? Nowhere to be found.

The other time people fled from Jesus was when he

spoke to them about the Eucharist. He said, "I am the bread of life . . . Unless you eat the flesh of the Son of Man and drink his blood, you have no life in you." (John 6:48, 53)

Immediately after this, we read in the Gospel: "When many of his disciples heard it, they said, 'This is a difficult teaching; who can accept it?'" (John 6:60) And a few lines later we read, "After this, many of his disciples turned back and no longer followed him." (John 6:66)

Notice Jesus didn't say, "Oh, come back. I was only kidding. Let's talk about it. Maybe I was wrong. Perhaps we can change this teaching. We can work something out." No, he turned to his disciples, just as he turns to you and me today, and said, "Do you also wish to leave me?"

Will you flee from Jesus or remain by his side?

The Eucharist is at the core of our faith. Let's explore what it is and what it means to you.

***

There are a lot of things I love about being Catholic, but at the top of the list is the Eucharist. Most people have never really stopped to think about it, but the Eucharist is amazing.

I was asked once: What would have to happen for you to leave the Catholic Church? I thought about the question for a long time. I combed through the lowest moments in Catholic history, testing each to see if one of them would have been the breaking point that made me leave. But after thinking it through I decided I could never leave the Catholic Church. The reason is because I believe that Jesus is truly present—body, blood, soul, and divinity—in the Eucharist. Where else can I get the Eucharist?

Sure, some other churches might have better music, but in the whole scheme of things music is trivial compared to the Eucharist. Other churches might have more engaging preachers, but these are trivial compared to the Eucharist. When we go to Mass on Sunday the danger is in thinking that the music and the homily are the most important things. Don't take the trivial and make it important. That's the way of the world. Get clear about what's really important, what matters most, and life will be a lot simpler and more joyful.

At Mass on Sunday, the homily could be in a language I don't understand, the music could be a complete train wreck, there could be kids running up and down the aisles screaming at the top of their lungs, throwing crayons and eating snacks (or eating crayons and throwing snacks), and that's OK—because the moment when I receive the Eucharist is a pivotal moment in my week. It's a moment of transformation, a moment when I get to receive who and what I wish to become. And I could never leave that. It doesn't matter how good the music or preaching is elsewhere; I cannot leave the Eucharist. I will not leave Jesus. I hope you won't either.

When I reflect on the gift of faith I have been given, I am led to the conclusion that once we believe in the Eucharist we are given the grace to look beyond a bad homily; the grace to look beyond uninspiring music and the grace to look beyond music that elevates our hearts, minds, and souls. For it is beyond all of these things, way beyond all these things, that we find Jesus in the Eucharist.

This sets the Catholic Church apart: Jesus truly present in the Eucharist. The Eucharist is uniquely Catholic.

Let me ask you a question. If you had to spend the rest of your life on a deserted island, and you could only take five people with you, whom would you take?

I can tell you a priest would be on my list of five people. No priest, no Mass. No Mass, no Eucharist. I can't live without the Eucharist. More importantly, I don't want to. And once you come to understand the power of the Eucharist, you won't want to either.

I was born Catholic and I will die Catholic. There are lots of reasons for that, but none more compelling than the Eucharist.

***

You might be thinking to yourself, "I'm not sure if I believe that Jesus is truly present in the host I receive at Mass on Sunday." You wouldn't be the first person to have doubts. Great faith and great doubt often go hand in hand. There was a priest who lived in Lanciano, Italy, around the year 700, who was plagued with doubts about the True Presence . . . until one day. After that day he never again doubted that Jesus was truly present in the Eucharist.

What happened on that day? I'm glad you asked.

On that day, the priest was celebrating Mass in the small church, even though he was filled with doubts about the Real Presence of Jesus in the Eucharist. As he said the Words of Consecration ("Take this, all of you, and eat of it, for this is my body which will be given up for you."), the bread changed into living flesh and the wine changed into blood before his eyes.

Today, you can go to Lanciano and see the flesh and blood that has remained there for more than thirteen hundred years. The flesh and blood have been studied by scientists on a number of occasions, and the following conclusions have been drawn: The flesh is real human flesh and the blood is real human blood, the flesh is muscular tissue from the heart, and there is no evidence of preservatives or any other chemical agents present.

This is one of thousands of Eucharistic miracles that have been documented throughout the life of the Church.

At the Last Supper Jesus "took the bread, and when he had given thanks, he broke it and gave it to them, saying, 'This is my body, which is given for you. Do this in remembrance of me.'" (Luke 22:19) We take Jesus at his word. At Mass on Sunday the priest extends his hands over simple bread and wine and asks the Holy Spirit to transform them into the body and blood of Jesus Christ.

If the Holy Spirit can do that to bread and wine, imagine what he can do with you if you open yourself up to the experience of Communion.

You are not just a body. You are a delicate composition of body and soul. If you haven't already, one day you will discover you need to feed your soul in order to live a full and happy life. And when that day comes I want you to remember today, because there is no better way to feed your soul than with the Eucharist.

The Eucharist is astonishing. God himself wants to nourish us. God himself wants to feed us spiritually. God wants to dwell in you.

Some people say that the bread and wine are just a symbol of Jesus' body and blood, but that is not what we believe as Catholics. And the evidence found in Divine Revelation suggests that it is not just a symbol. The Scriptures don't suggest a symbol. Jesus didn't say, "Unless you eat a symbol of my flesh and drink a symbol of my blood you will not have life." And remember there are two aspects of Divine Revelation: Scripture and Tradition. And from the earliest times, Christians have believed that the Eucharist was the body and blood of the Risen Jesus, and not just a symbol.

Can I prove it to you scientifically? No. Not everything can be explained or proven scientifically. If you could prove everything scientifically, there would be no need for faith. There is such a thing as mystery. We human beings don't know everything. If we did, we would be God, and there is plenty of evidence in our daily lives that confirms that human beings are not God. Life is full of mystery, and mystery is a beautiful thing.

At the heart of the mystery that is the Catholic faith is the Eucharist. I hope with every passing year of your life you will explore and embrace the mystery of the Eucharist more.

The wiser you become, the closer you will want to be to God. And God wants to be close to us. St. Francis de Sales wrote, "In the Eucharist we become one with God." To be one with God is a beautiful thing, and whether you are aware of it or not, it is your deepest yearning. You have an insatiable yearning to be one with God. I hope you will start listening to that yearning.

If you want to have a life-changing experience, find an Adoration Chapel in your area and visit it. Sit there in Jesus' presence for one hour. You will be amazed how powerful Jesus' presence is, and how much he will teach you about yourself and your life in one hour.

***

When was the last time you did something that you

knew wasn't good for you? Why did you do it? Think of reasons, come up with excuses, but at the end of the day it comes down to this: You have disordered desires that are very difficult to control.

Have you ever tried to quit a bad habit and failed? If you haven't already, the day will come when you will try to end a self-destructive habit and find yourself powerless over it. You will use all the willpower you can summon, but you will find yourself failing over and over again. These moments in life can be very humbling—and that's good, because they make us realize our need for God and his grace.

Grace is the assistance God gives us to do what is good, true, noble, and right. And there is no better way to receive God's grace than through the Eucharist.

There is a lot of talk these days about superfoods. Superfoods are high in nutrients and rich with antioxidants, and they keep your immune system strong to fight off disease. Some examples include pomegranate juice, salmon, alfalfa sprouts, sweet potatoes, kale, prunes, beets, apples, and beans.

The Eucharist is the ultimate superfood for the soul, loaded with grace to keep you spiritually healthy, give you the wisdom and strength to choose the right path, and fight off diseases like selfishness and other related vices and bad habits. And that is just a tiny fraction of the power the Eucharist holds.

When you go to Mass next Sunday, keep in mind, the Eucharist is not just a symbol. This is Jesus. The same Jesus who healed people with a touch. The same man who taught with more wisdom than any person who ever walked the earth. This is the guy who fed five thousand people with five loaves and two fishes. The same Jesus who rose from the dead.

We've all got problems. We all have struggles. But whatever you've got, he can handle. You need grace. You may not know it yet, but the sooner you realize it the better. And the Eucharist is the supreme source of the grace you need.

Isn't it time you allowed God to unleash the power of grace in your life?

1. MASS WAS BORING… UNTIL THIS HAPPENED

— Jackie Francois Angel —

Growing up as a nominal, lukewarm Catholic, I thought Mass was boring.

As an elementary-aged student, I remember falling asleep on my mom's lap while listening to the cantor's wobbly, out-of-tune voice and staring at the stained-glass windows with my heavy eyelids as my sister repeatedly tapped the fabric-padded kneeler with her shaky, anxious foot.

As I went through junior high and high school, our catechism classes and youth ministry offered "teaching Masses." The priest would pause between different moments in the Mass to explain what was happening, why he did what he did in that moment, and the meaning of the prayers. This piqued my interest a little bit, but without an active, living relationship with Jesus, it was like learning about another history fact, no different than the political figures I was learning about in school. I could appreciate the sentiment behind the Mass, just as a non-religious tourist could walk through the Sistine Chapel and appreciate the artwork and history.

But the summer after senior year of high school, I attended a retreat and everything changed.

While I had been to many retreats and conferences in high school (and even a World Youth Day in Rome), this was different. I was in a different place (both physically and spiritually), I was surrounded by 30 other high schoolers from around the country that I didn't know, and there were a few things I had never experienced. On this particular week-long retreat that led up to a Steubenville youth conference, I encountered a few things that changed my life.

The first was the other high schoolers who were with me. As an 18-year-old, I watched these younger students talk about their Catholic faith in a way that was alive with joy, deep wisdom, and knowledge. I thought, "How can I have been Catholic my whole life, but I have no clue what these people are talking about? What's a 'Divine Mercy Chaplet?' What's a 'Padre Pio?' What the heck does 'NFP' stand for?" I felt like they were speaking a new language and I was the deer in headlights cluelessly nodding along. Meanwhile, God was stirring in my heart a desire for more than I had ever known.

Second, we went to daily Mass (which I had never experienced, let alone for a week straight), and we had multiple encounters with Jesus in Eucharistic Adoration, where we would spend time singing, praying, journaling, and being in silence. That week stirred a zeal in me: I didn't want to be 50% Catholic anymore. I didn't want to be ignorant of my faith. I didn't want to be Catholic just to follow a "bunch of rules" or because my mom made me. I wanted a relationship with Jesus for all eternity.

When I came home from that retreat, I started going to daily Mass during the summer at 8 am. While it seemed I was the only person under 80-years-old at daily Mass, I didn't care. I wanted to receive Jesus as much as possible, and I wanted to learn everything I could about Him. I started reading every book and document and teaching of the Church I could get my hands on, whether it was about the Eucharist, apologetics, the sacraments, or the saints. I started memorizing Scripture. I even started writing music about my newfound love for Jesus.

While I didn't know St. Anselm's motto, "Faith seeking understanding," I was living it. It felt like everything I learned the first 18 years of my life went in one ear and out the other. But now that I actually had a love for Jesus, my faith propelled me to seek answers, and this time they stuck.

As I learned about the Mass with new ears and a new heart, my mind reveled in the beauty, truth, and goodness of it all. While I had received Jesus thousands of times in the Eucharist in my first 18 years of life, my eyes were opened to this beautiful covenant relationship where Jesus was the Bridegroom and I was His bride. I learned that every Mass is a wedding feast, a foretaste of the eternal wedding feast of Heaven, and that the Eucharist is where we become one flesh with God, our Beloved.

Cardinal Ratzinger (the future Pope Benedict XVI) wrote in his book *The Spirit of the Liturgy*, "In the Eucharist a communion takes place that corresponds to the union of man and woman in marriage. Just as they become 'one flesh,' so in Communion we all become 'one spirit,' one person, with Christ."

How amazing that we become ONE with GOD when receiving the Eucharist! Out of all the possible forms of intimacy with God—reading His Word in Scripture, praying in silence, singing in praise, gazing at His face in Eucharistic Adoration—THIS becoming ONE is the greatest. In fact, as the Catholic Church says, it is the "source and summit of the Christian life" (CCC 1324) because the Eucharist is Jesus Himself, Body, Blood, Soul, and Divinity. The Catholic Church says it is called "*Holy Communion*, because by this sacrament we unite ourselves to Christ, who makes us sharers in His Body and Blood to form a single body" (CCC 1331). How beautiful!

While the first years of my life were spent in ignorance of this glorious reality, I know I will spend the rest of my life pondering, learning, and savoring the Mass, and being in complete awe and gratitude that I get to participate in this covenant of love.

QUOTE: "The happiness you are seeking, the happiness you have a right to enjoy has a name and a face: it is Jesus of Nazareth, hidden in the Eucharist." Pope Benedict XVI

POINT TO PONDER: When you embrace a deep, dynamic and personal relationship with Jesus in the Eucharist, your entire life will be transformed.

VERSE TO LIVE: "Come to me, all you that are weary and are carrying heavy burdens, and I will give you rest. Take my yoke upon you, and learn from me; for I am gentle and humble in heart, and you will find rest for your souls. For my yoke is easy, and my burden is light." Matthew 11: 28-30

PRAYER: Jesus, give me the courage to let down my guard, the grace to stop resisting you in all the ways I do, and the wisdom to make time to sit in your presence each day. Amen.

JACKIE FRANCOIS ANGEL is a faith-based speaker, singer/songwriter, worship leader, and host of the *@JackieFrancois* YouTube channel. Alongside her husband, she is the author of *Forever: A Catholic Devotional for Your Marriage.*

WANT TO GROW SPIRITUALLY?

Read *Walk Softly and Carry a Great Bag*

by Teresa Tomeo

and

Jesus, Present Before Me

by Fr. Peter John Cameron

2. WHY DO YOU DO THAT?

— Father Mike Schmitz —

I went to a college where everyone would gather around the altar during Mass. For the Eucharist, they had bread that was substantial, rather than the dried crispy wafer. When people distributed the Eucharist they would rip off pieces of the bread—the body—and hand them to you. The unfortunate thing was that after Mass, all around the altar on the ground were all these crumbs of the Eucharist.

I remember in my years of college, there was always this one guy. He was in my class and he was kind of a big man on campus. He was an athlete and everyone loved him. He was super funny. After everyone would leave Mass and we'd all be in the back of the church, this guy would be up around the altar on his hands and knees eating the crumbs of the Eucharist off the floor. I remember being in the back like, *Dude that's weird. You're making a spectacle of yourself.* But after a while I finally asked him, "Dude, why do you do that?"

He said when he was 15 years old, he heard a story:

When the Communists came into power in China, one of the things they wanted to do was suppress religion, especially Christianity. At one point they came to this village, took the priest, and locked him in the house next to the church. And then they went into the church and just destroyed the place. They turned over pews and they ripped the Bible.

The priest was sitting at the window, looking out of his rectory, watching helplessly as they destroyed the church.

At one point these soldiers took the tabernacle and they threw it out the window. It crashed through the window, hit the ground, and exploded open. The Eucharist fell out and scattered on the ground. Jesus' body, this body that was given for him, was discarded on the ground.

Because the priest was under house arrest, all he could do was stand there and keep watch with Jesus. So, he stood there, with the Eucharist on the ground outside his window.

As night fell, he saw this figure getting closer and clos-

er. Darting from shadow to shadow. And as it got closer, he recognized it was a 12-year-old girl from his parish. She had seen what the soldiers had done and she had seen the Eucharist on the ground. So she waited until night fell and she snuck to the Eucharist. She was taught as a kid not to touch the Eucharist with your hands, so she knelt down and bent her face to the ground. She picked up the Eucharist off the ground with her tongue, stood up, and made the Sign of the Cross. She was also taught you only receive Communion once, so she got up and then she snuck away into the night.

The priest knew exactly how many consecrated hosts of the body of Christ were there. Night after night this girl kept coming back. She'd sneak toward the abandoned hosts, kneel down, and receive the Eucharist off the ground, make the Sign of the Cross, get up and run away into the night—until the last night.

He knew it was the last time and he knew that after this she'd be safe. After this she wouldn't have to keep coming back and risking her life.

That last night, he saw her approaching as he was praying. She came closer and closer, knelt down, and she received Jesus off the ground with her tongue, and made the Sign of the Cross. This beautiful ritual brought the priest to tears.

But, as the girl got up, she knocked something over and a

noise echoed through the night. Her heart skipped a beat, and the priest's heart was seized with fear for the girl's safety.

Two soldiers rushed to where she was. They saw what she was doing and they beat the 12-year-old girl to death with the butts of their rifles.

After telling me the story, this guy looked at me and he said, "Why do I do this? That's why. Because one drop of the precious blood of Jesus is enough to save the world. And one crumb of the body of Jesus is enough to save the world. So why do I eat the crumbs of Jesus off the ground? Because I cannot do otherwise. Because He gives His whole self to me. I cannot but give my whole self to Him."

QUOTE: "This morning my soul is greater than the world since it possesses You, You whom heaven and earth do not contain." Saint Margaret of Cortona

POINT TO PONDER: When was the last time you did something wholeheartedly? Jesus gives his whole self to you in the Eucharist. How would your life change if you gave your whole self to him?

VERSE TO LIVE: "I know what it is to have little, and I know what it is to have plenty. In any and all circumstances I have learned the secret of being well-fed and of going hungry, of having plenty and of being in need. I can do all things through him who strengthens me." Philippians 4:12-13

PRAYER: Lord, take the blindness from my eyes, the hardness from my heart, and draw me nearer to you than ever before. Amen.

FATHER MIKE SCHMITZ is the author of *How to Make Great Decisions*. He currently runs the Newman Center at the University of Minnesota-Duluth and is also the Director of Youth and Young Adult Ministry for the diocese. This reflection was adapted from Father Mike Schmitz's talk at the SEEK2015 Conference.

WANT TO GROW SPIRITUALLY?

Read *How to Make Great Decisions*

by Father Mike Schmitz

and

Understanding the Mass: 100 Questions 100 Answers

by Mike Aquilina

3. DO YOU KNOW WHERE YOU'RE GOING?

— Lisa M. Hendey —

To say that I first fell in love with the Eucharist before my conscious memories had taken shape is not an exaggeration. My parents were high school sweethearts, lifelong Hoosiers who married just weeks after their college graduation. When I arrived in June of 1963, two months before their first anniversary, they placed me and a few possessions in the backseat of their car and headed West to join friends in California. Lifelong Catholics, Mom and Daddy made sure I was baptized in Indiana before embarking on what they assumed would be a one or two-year adventure.

Around that same time, a small parish in Southern California was being seeded by a young Irish pastor.

Father Michael Collins' vocational calling had carried him from County Limerick in war-torn Europe to the mission territory of Orange County. As my parents drove West, Father was galvanizing the faithful in his territorial boundaries to transform a ten-acre tomato patch into a vibrant church and Catholic school. My parents found our new church "home" long before they could afford their first house. At St. Barbara's, our family grew into what would soon be five children. As much as the suburban house they eventually bought was home, so was St. Barbara's.

A child of the sixties, my earliest memories of Mass include both a communion rail and the singing of popular songs that could somehow be related to the Gospel themes Father Collins was preaching each Sunday. My education in the faith fell not only to my parents but to two wildly disparate orders of religious Sisters. My first teachers, the habited Poor Clare Missionary Sisters from Mexico, were strict and exacting. Their eventual replacements, the Sisters of St. Francis from Syracuse, New York, arrived at our school in the seventies with skateboards and guitars. These holy women who loved Christ and our community embodied the spirit and zeal of the Vatican II teachings which were being promulgated worldwide.

From the Poor Clares, I learned spiritual discipline and intentional generosity. From the Franciscans, I learned that God loved me unconditionally and that our Church needed my gifts and participation, even in my childhood. From Father Collins, I learned that Scripture was meant to be read, shared, and lived. Father taught us that Mass was a vibrant act of worship, and that the Eucharist was the True Presence of Jesus Christ. In my childhood brain, I assumed God had an Irish accent like the priest who loved Him with greater ferocity than any other love I knew. I'm still not convinced that God doesn't sound just like that Irish priest who led thousands of families to know and love the Eucharist and one another.

Father Collins' love for the Mass transformed our parish from people who spent one hour a week at church into missionaries called to live the Church's social teachings. As a young girl, I became involved in music ministry and often attended Mass two or three times on Sundays, always anxious to serve. Our after-Mass family respites on Sunday afternoons included a famous "Mass

Quiz Question" game where Daddy tested our comprehension while Mom took a needed break. Father's deep love for the Rosary permeated our family culture. But far from being rote prayer, our familial recitation of the decades tied us to an ever-deepening love for Jesus and a trust in the intercession of His Mother. At St. Barbara's, loving the Eucharist meant loving and caring for one another and anyone we met who was in need.

When I arrived at Mater Dei High School in the fall of 1977, my love for Mass and the Eucharist was deepened. As students, we planned daily Communion Services, ministering to one another with word and song and receiving the Eucharist. Receiving Jesus in Holy Communion before lunch each day was as much a part of my routine at Mater Dei as going to my locker or visiting with friends. When I matriculated at the University of Notre Dame in 1981, that routine continued. It was easy and fun to participate in daily Mass in the crypt of the beautiful basilica or in one of the many dorms on campus where nighttime Mass was offered. My study abroad experiences afforded me the chance to visit the great sanctuaries of Europe, the first of many places worldwide where I would receive the Eucharist and worship. Despite my inability to understand some of the languages spoken in those cities, I knew I was "home."

Even after years of religion classes and college-level theology, my faith was as simple as that of my chosen patron saint, Thérèse of Lisieux. I loved Jesus. I loved Mass. I loved what I believed the Eucharist to be: Jesus Christ, body, and soul, living within my heart. I did not have profound formal terminologies to explain the precepts of my faith. But I knew beyond a doubt that Jesus was truly present in the Eucharist. And so, I longed to experience that gift daily, despite the many ways in which I knew I fell short of worthiness for such grace. Father Collins' teachings, my parents' simple yet sound example, and the environment around me at Notre Dame stoked my vibrant, yet untested confidence in God's mercy and love.

I was soon a twenty-two-year-old woman standing before the altar at the Basilica of the Sacred Heart marrying the man of my dreams. When Greg and I met and fell in love during our senior year at Notre Dame, the fact that he was not Catholic didn't register as a concern for me. We participated in a great deal of Pre-Cana preparation, discussing how we would cooperate mutually in raising our children in the Catholic faith while Greg would continue to discern his own spiritual path. I had no real sense of what that meant. I simply trusted that my love for my faith and this amazing man would be enough, and that God would help us to find a way forward.

Looking back over thirty-five plus years since our beloved Father Collins led us through our profession of those marriage vows, I can see how our trust in God's plan and my abiding love for Christ's True Presence in the Eucharist have sustained me.

My immature faith survived the early years when I judged my husband for what I perceived to be his shortcomings as Greg himself eventually found his way to the Church and the Eucharistic table in God's time, not Lisa's. It turns out that the person who truly needed to know Christ more fully was me. When I stopped judging Greg's journey to Jesus and began to prioritize my own, grace poured into our marriage. My faith in God's love has enabled me to accept that Greg's journey and that of our sons, their wives, and our grandchildren are uniquely their own and not mine to guide, control, or dictate. I will always pray for them. But their path to the Divine is their own to travel.

My fragile faith has also withstood the untimely passing of my parents, far too early and within months of one another. I believe with certainty that they now rest forever in the arms of our Savior, that their joy is complete in the light of God's face.

My story has simple beginnings, complex middle chapters, and an ending yet waiting to be written. Despite my occasional frustrations with the machinations of the institutional Church and the misdeeds of her people, myself included, I remain fully, inexorably bound to the gift of Jesus Christ, truly present in the Eucharist. I fall short of having words adequate to describe this blessing, so I often turn to those of the saints. When friends of different faiths or those who have been separated from the Church question me or attempt debate, I simply ask them to pray for me, that I may be worthy of the bountiful love God shares with me. And I share that I hope that they too will experience this love.

Loving God and being loved by God is not a magic bullet that helps us avoid suffering or hardship in our lives. At times, my heart is so full of varying emotions after having received Communion that I am moved to silent tears.

The Eucharist is not a potion for power or a portal to the perfect life. It is, rather, a balm, a warm hug, an indescribable gift that compels us to, in turn, give to those around us. In receiving Jesus, especially in our brokenness and need, we are called to a generative love. We are God's beloved in a world that is greatly in need of the very gifts Jesus Christ came to give. Through, with, and in Him, hope overflows.

QUOTE: "The most deadly poison of our times is indifference. And this happens although the praise of God should know no limits. Let us strive therefore to praise him to the greatest extent of our powers." Saint Maximilian Kolbe

POINT TO PONDER: Every chapter of your life so far has been touched by God's grace, even if you couldn't see it at the time.

VERSE TO LIVE: "'For I know the plans I have for you,' declares the Lord, 'plans to prosper you and not to harm you, plans to give you a hope and a future.'" Jeremiah 29:11

PRAYER: Lord, open my eyes to see the ways you have moved in my life in the past, so that I may have faith that you are moving in my life today, and hope that you will continue to move in my life in the future. Amen.

LISA M. HENDEY is the founder and editor of the Catholic Mom blog and the bestselling author of *The Grace of Yes: Eight Virtues for Generous Living* and *The Handbook for Catholic Moms.* She travels internationally, giving workshops on faith and family, and is a regular guest on television and radio shows.

WANT TO GROW SPIRITUALLY?

Read

77 Ways to Pray with Your Kids

by Jerry Windley-Daoust

and

Wrapped Up! God's Ten Gifts for Women

by Teresa Tomeo and Cheryl Dickow

4. WHAT I LEARNED FROM A MUSLIM ABOUT THE EUCHARIST

— *Peter Kreeft* —

Most Catholics probably don't think they can learn anything about the Eucharist from a Muslim, or people of other faiths in general. This is the story of what I learned.

We do, said John.

Your Church teaches that He is really present there, yes? That what's there is the man who was God?

Yes. The formula is 'body and blood, soul and divinity.'

And you believe that?

Yes.

Isa made as if to say something, but stifled it. John assured him he would not be offended.

Finally, reluctantly, Isa said, *I don't understand.*

I understand how you feel. It sounds very shocking.

No, you don't understand. That's not what I mean. You will take it as an insult, but I don't mean it to be.

I promise I won't take it as an insult. But I really want to know what's on your mind.

Well then . . . I don't think you really do believe that. I don't mean to say you're dishonest, but . . .

I think I know what you mean. You can't empathize with anyone who believes something so shocking. You don't see how you could ever get down on your knees before that altar.

No, I don't see how I could ever get up. If I believed that thing that looks like a little round piece of bread was really Allah Himself, I think I would just faint. I would fall at His feet like a dead man.

John looked carefully at my reaction as he reported Isa's words. My eyes opened, and he smiled. "What did you say to him?" I asked.

"Nothing. Then, after a while, just 'Yes.'"

John is a wise man.

This story got me thinking about the ills of our culture both outside and inside the Church. Every American knows our culture is in crisis. And every Catholic knows that the crisis has infected the Church as well as the world. But what is the root of the disease? As St. Thomas Aquinas says, the primary object of faith is a reality, not a proposition (though propositions are indispensable). Not the proposition God exists, but God; not the doctrine of the Resurrection, but the reality of the Resurrection; not the creeds about Christ, but the real presence of Christ, is the crux and crisis. It is a crisis of Christlessness.

The crisis of faith in the Church is a crisis of faith in Christ's real presence. The deepest root of the dullness and ineffectiveness of most parishes, laity, clergy, homilies, liturgies, music, catechesis, programs, and all the extra Martha-like activities is not outright heresy or apostasy, but simply remoteness from The Person.

Let's ask ourselves honestly: Why have Evangelical, Fundamentalist, and Pentecostal Protestant sects and denominations been so much more successful throughout the Americas during the past generation? Why would a Catholic, who is in possession of the fullness of the faith, the full Gospel, exchange it for a faith that is only partial? It is not primarily because of a disaffection for the things Catholics have and Protestants don't: history, tradition, popes, saints, sacraments, etc. Rather, it is due to an affection for the one thing Catholics have but don't know they have—in fact, the main thing Catholics have: Christ. These Catholics never knew Jesus Christ in the Church, but they did find Christ present in the souls and lives of Protestants.

Ironically, the Church has a presence these Protestants do not even claim to have: an objective and perfect real presence in the Eucharist, worthy of worship, not just a subjective and imperfect presence in souls. Christ is really, truly, objectively, fully present in the Eucharist, hidden under the appearances of bread and wine, as He was in the streets of Nazareth or on the Cross.

And that's what we're neglecting!

The central problem of the Church today is that most of the generation now becoming adults, the generation educated by CCD texts full of deadly platitudes, simply do not know Jesus Christ. They are not merely unaware of right doctrine about Him (though that's tragically missing too), but of Christ Himself, His real presence. Nothing less than Christ could have Christianized the world, nothing less than Christlessness has de-Christianized it, and nothing less than Christ can re-Christianize it. What happens when Christ's real presence is known? Read the Gospels and find out. The Gospels are not mere historical records; they continue, they happen, for the One they present is not dead and gone and past, but alive and here and now.

Where is He present now? In His Church. This means essentially two things. First, He is present in the Church's sacraments, primarily in the Eucharist. Second, He is also present in the Church's members, in the souls and lives of those who have believed in Him. What a tragedy that so many Protestants do not know that first presence! And what an equal tragedy that so many Catholics do not know the second!

What will happen if we also neglect the first? What sound will we hear to replace the great silence of Eucharistic Adoration? The same sound we hear from the National Council of Churches: the sound of coffins being built, the sound of dead logs falling.

And what will we hear if we rediscover His presence and adore Him? The same sound we hear in the Gospels: the sound of a blazing fire, the rattle of dry bones coming to life, the shouts of joy that ring through Scripture and through the great old Protestant hymns.

How do we get this joy back? Not by any gimmicks

or human contrivance, but by recognizing the real presence and responding with adoration. And the primary place of the real presence is the Eucharist.

What holds us back, then? What is the objection to Eucharistic Adoration? It's not that it's hard or requires any special gifts or education. The only requirements are faith and love.

How does that mean you can help the Church and the world by sitting in a dark building doing nothing? You can't. But you can mightily help both by doing something: adoring Christ, who is really present there in the Eucharist.

But what do you do when you adore? You let God do things. He forms our minds and hearts if we give them to Him.

That sounds Quietist, or Buddhist. Buddhists often understand the superior power of silence over speech, and of contemplation over action, better than Catholics do today. By serving a cup of green tea, I stopped the war.

How can drinking tea stop war? By changing souls, which are the sources of war. By touching the root, not the branches.

What does that have to do with Eucharistic Adoration? There too we touch the root, the root of everything, Christ the Pantocrator. And when we touch this root, the root of all life with our own root, our heart, we touch our candle to His fire. We touch a power infinitely greater than nuclear power, the Sun, or the Big Bang.

What power is that? The Blood and Body of Christ.

QUOTE: "All the answers are in the tabernacle." Matthew Kelly

POINT TO PONDER: Every problem you face can be solved by Jesus' presence. Invite Him to participate in the events of your life.

VERSE TO LIVE: "Let the same mind be in you that was in Christ Jesus, who, though he was in the form of God, did not regard equality with God as something to be exploited, but emptied himself, taking the form of a slave, being born in human likeness. And being found in human form, he humbled himself and became obedient to the point of death—even death on a cross." Philippians 2:5-8

PRAYER: Lord, unite all men and women of faith around

the world, so that together, despite our differences and disagreements, we can fight against the evil that seeks to steal from our children and their children the right to worship. Amen.

PETER KREEFT is the author of *Jesus Shock, Making Sense out of Suffering,* and *Making Choices: Practical Wisdom for Everyday Moral Decisions.* He is a beloved Professor of Philosophy at Boston College and a renowned speaker. This reflection was adapted from his article: *What I Learned from a Muslim about Eucharistic Adoration.*

WANT TO GROW SPIRITUALLY?

Read

Jesus Shock

by Peter Kreeft

and

Rediscover Jesus

by Matthew Kelly

5. COME AWAY TO A QUIET PLACE

— Jenna Greiwe —

My faith came to life my freshman year of high school. There were a handful of people who were part of creating that spark, but none as much as Angie.

Angie was the youth minister at my local parish and she brought Jesus to life for me. Every Sunday she told me that Jesus Christ loved me, and if I was the only person who had ever lived, Jesus still would have died for me.

I didn't fully appreciate it at the time, but hearing her tell me that over and over again was a powerful force in my life.

I used to wonder how Angie knew that Jesus loved me that much and how she could say it with such conviction. I certainly didn't share her confidence at the time. My faith was shallow. Almost everything else in my life was a priority over my relationship with Jesus. What could Angie see that I couldn't? What was she aware of that I was missing?

I didn't have to look far to figure out how Angie was able to believe so strongly. At least once a month, she would bring our youth group to pray together in front of the Blessed Sacrament in Adoration. Dozens of kids knelt and sat in front of the altar.

It was a sight to behold. In a world of busyness and noise, with ever-growing distractions like phones and social media, there were a bunch of teenagers spending time in silence and stillness. Angie was our guide in these deep waters. As I look back now, I realize Angie lived out Jesus' call to "Come away to a quiet place" better than maybe anyone I've ever known.

It was there in the quiet place of Adoration that Angie showed me how to connect with Jesus on a deeper and more personal level than I ever thought possible. I'll never forget the words she spoke on our group's first trip to the chapel.

"Just picture Jesus as if He's sitting up there on the altar—because He is. He's just talking to you and you're talking to Him. What does He want to tell you? What do you want to say to Him?"

It sounds simple, but that changed everything for me. The more time I spent with Jesus in the Eucharist, the more personal His presence became. And the fruits that flooded my life after each visit were obvious: stillness, calm, prayer, and joy. In the midst of chaos and problems and anxiety, there was Jesus.

Something else started happening too. After each time going to Adoration, the very next time I received the Eucharist on Sunday was a radically more meaningful experience. Of course that makes total sense now, but experiencing it then was like being shown a secret I had been missing right in front of me my entire life. Jesus was really there, in that tiny white host.

That deepening process continued for about two years until finally I felt ready to take the next step. It was my junior year of high school when I first decided to visit a church on my own and spend time with Jesus totally by myself. I remember stepping into that completely empty church. The silence was deafening and refreshing all at once. I remembered Angie's advice and just pictured Jesus up on the altar and started talking. Nothing extraordinary happened. No major revelations. I simply found the peace and calm I always did. But making that choice to seek out Jesus in a quiet place myself . . . that was the moment I truly made the faith my own.

In the years since, finding the time and energy to seek out a quiet place has become more difficult. A lot has changed. I'm a mom. I'm a wife. I have a full-time job. The world has changed. It's even noisier and more chaotic than it was then.

But that's exactly why now, more than ever, I need the clarity and peace Adoration provides. So I do what I can. When I can't find time alone, I bring my son with me and try to teach him that Jesus is there. On busy days, I try to just spend five minutes with Jesus in a quiet chapel. Because even that little dose of silence and stillness is enough to keep me going.

Without that time with Jesus, my life would fall apart so quickly it would make your head spin. I seriously mean that. Nine times out of ten when my life gets taken over by confusion, anxiety and overwhelm, I can trace it back to one thing: I haven't been seeking out Jesus in the quiet of Adoration. As soon as I return, my problems don't simply disappear, but peace becomes possible again, and, more often than not, the next right step becomes clear.

So here's my encouragement for you. Whenever you are filled with worry, desperate for hope, looking for clarity, or just need a moment of peace, go to a quiet place and visit Jesus in the Eucharist. Just talk to Him like He's sitting on the altar.

He'll give you exactly what you need.

QUOTE: "We become what we love and who we love shapes what we become." Saint Clare of Assisi

POINT TO PONDER: We live in a busy and noisy world, but don't blindly accept that your life has no choice but to be busy and noisy. Seek the rest that silence naturally brings to your heart, mind, body, and soul.

VERSE TO LIVE: "And he said to them, 'Come away by yourselves to a quiet place, and rest a while.' For many were coming and going, and they had no leisure even to eat." Mark 6:31

PRAYER: Lord, whenever I am filled with worry, desperate for hope, looking for clarity, or just need a moment of peace, remind me to visit you in the Eucharist. Draw me to that quiet place where I just know you will give me exactly what I need. Amen.

JENNA GREIWE has been a dedicated member of the Dynamic Catholic team for more than 12 years. During that time, she has served the ministry and mission in a number of key roles, and, together with her colleagues, reaches tens of millions of people each year with a message of hope and inspiration.

WANT TO GROW SPIRITUALLY?

Read
The Mindful Catholic:
Finding God One Moment at a Time
by Dr. Gregory Bottaro
and
Stop Worrying and Start Living
by Gary Zimak

6. RIGHT HERE, RIGHT NOW, NO OTHER PLACE I'D RATHER BE!

— Bishop Andrew Cozzens —

Why is it so important that we hand on the teaching of the Real Presence of Jesus in the Eucharist? When someone experiences that Jesus is really present in the Eucharist, it helps them to understand what it means to be a disciple.

So what's a disciple? A student. A learner. Someone who has come to understand what we see in the Gospels, which is that *Jesus is Lord.* The early Christians loved that phrase, "Jesus is Lord." And it captured for them the essence of discipleship. What does that mean? Jesus is the center of my life. Jesus is the first person in my life. And my life is directed toward him.

Today, the vision that the world gives us for happiness is basically that we have to get everything right. If I go to the right college and I get the right job, and then I find the right spouse and I get the right friends, and then I live in the right place—if I get all that right, then I'll be happy. It's no wonder we all have so much anxiety. Because that's a lot of stuff to try to get right. What's the problem with this picture? Well, the problem is that I'm at the center, and I'll never get all that right, and no one of those things will ever satisfy me. And so, in order to be happy, what do I have to do? I have to dethrone myself from the center of my life, put Jesus at the center, and then ask Him: *Jesus, where do you want me to go to college? What's the career you made me for? Who am I supposed to marry, if I'm supposed to get married? What's my vocation?* All those questions come when I realize Jesus is Lord.

But a very powerful thing can happen in a person's life when they experience the Real Presence of Jesus in the Eucharist, because then the Lord is real, and He's right here before me. I've seen it happen so many times.

I remember once I was at a conference with some young people from my parish. I was a parish priest at the time, and I had one particular young person who didn't want to be there. He was only there because his parents made him come. So he was resistant. We were getting ready for the Adoration time on Saturday night and he was sitting there with his head down, so I felt inspired by the Holy Spirit and I went up to him.

I said, "God wants to do something in you tonight."

He was like, "Eh, I don't know." And he kept his arms folded.

Well, at the end of the evening, after the Eucharist had come out and been processed around the stadium, that young man came up to me.

He said, "How did you know?"

I didn't know—I knew Jesus.

[That night, that young man] experienced that Jesus was really present in the Eucharist, and all of a sudden, all of his defenses went down. All of his heart was opened. He met the Lord, and he understood, this is God before me. Discipleship became a real thing like, *Okay, how do I orient my life if Jesus is really the Lord and if He's here right now?*

That can happen in lots of different ways. But one of the profound ways is through an experience of Jesus' presence in the Eucharist. What a difference that makes when you begin to sense in your heart His presence!

It's important to understand the heart of our Catholic teaching, which is simple, even though it's mysterious. And the simple truth is this: the substance of the bread and wine changes completely through the words of consecration, such that there's no more bread and wine there. It appears like bread and wine. It has all the properties of bread and wine, but there's no more bread and wine there. What *is* there? Jesus.

And He's present so that He can come to you because He wants to be one with you. There's no more intimate way that He could come to you except to come to you as your food, to feed your soul.

We need to be clear about that teaching. But it's not just teaching that makes a disciple. What we need is to move the heart.

And so we need to provide experiences where people can come to encounter Him—Adoration, devotions, music, the environment, candle-lit processions. Something beautiful that we're doing that helps us in our hearts because we're embodied persons. We're not just intellects. When we kneel, when we bow before Him, when we sing, all this helps us as embodied persons to experience His presence.

That's what changes hearts.

QUOTE: "Lord, I leave the past in Your mercy, the future in Your providential care and the present moment in Your Love." Saint Padre Pio

POINT TO PONDER: Jesus wants to do something in your heart right now. Will you let him? Bring whatever uncertainty you are currently facing to Jesus in the Eucharist and ask: *Jesus, what do you think I should do?*

VERSE TO LIVE: "The Lord is my rock, my fortress, and my deliverer, my God, my rock in whom I take refuge, my shield, and the horn of my salvation, my stronghold." Psalm 18:2

PRAYER: Right here, right now, there is no other place I would rather be, Lord, than in your presence. Right here, right now, there is no other place I would rather be, Lord, than in your presence. Right here, right now, there is no other place I would rather be, Lord, than in your presence. Amen.

BISHOP ANDREW COZZENS serves the Diocese of Crookston. He has also worked as a traveling missionary, professor, and religious educator. He was appointed to lead the three-year National Eucharistic Revival taking place in the United States at this time. This reflection was adapted from Bishop Andrew Cozzens' keynote address at the 2022 Joshua Congress.

WANT TO GROW SPIRITUALLY?

Read

Do Something Beautiful for God:

The Essential Teachings of Mother Teresa

by Mother Teresa

7. YOUR MOST URGENT NEED

— Fulton Sheen —

The whole world really has a hunger for God. As Augustine put it, "Our hearts were made for thee, O Lord, and they are restless until they rest in thee."

When our Blessed Lord saw a very hungry crowd, He said, I am sorry for the multitude for they have nothing to eat. What He gave them on that occasion is the subject of this lesson and it brings us to the Sacrament of the Eucharist.

The Eucharist is the greatest of all the sacraments because it contains in a substantial way the person of Christ, who is the author of life. If life is or if life is ever to live, it must nourish itself. If divine life is to live, it too needs its nourishment. That is the Eucharist.

All life lives through communion with some other

form of life. There's nothing on this earth that does not obey that law in some way or other. Take for example plant life. Though it does not commune with another kind of life, nevertheless, it is dependent upon something else for its existence. So the plant life will go down to the earth for water and for phosphates and carbonates, and it also draws much light from the Sun. If these chemicals were blotted out and the Sun were blotted out so as to deprive plant life of communion, it would perish.

When we get to animal life the law becomes far more clear. There's still greater need of nourishment. It needs, of course, nourishment from the mineral order like sunlight, air, and so forth, but the nourishment of the animal comes from plant life. From the very moment the animal comes into being, there is a quest for nourishment. Its fundamental instinct is to seek food. The animal roaming in the field, the fish swimming in the ocean, the eagle in the air—all are in search of daily bread. Without ever knowing it, they acknowledge the law that life is impossible without nourishment, that life grows only by life, and the joy of living comes from communion with another kind of life.

Now when you come to man, the same law applies. He has a body just as animals do, and that body clamors for food and more delicate food. Our body is not content as the plant to take its food from the ground, raw, uncooked, and unseasoned. It seeks the refinement that comes from a higher creature and in doing so acknowledges that universal law of life, that every living thing must nourish itself. Life lives by life and the joy of living is enhanced by communion with another form of life.

But here we come to a difference. Man is the soul as well as the body. Does not his soul demand food? And since his soul is spiritual, does it not require some spiritual food? There's nothing on this earth that can completely satisfy this soul hunger of man, simply because it is an unearthly hunger. Everything in this universe demands a nourishment that is suited to its nature. A canary does not use the same kind of food as a boa constrictor because its nature is different. Man's soul is spiritual and therefore it demands a spiritual food. Now what will that food be? Well, that question was answered by our Blessed Lord.

He who said that He was the Bread of Life, now in the words of the Gospel, took bread and blessed and broke it and gave it to them saying, this is my body given for you. Notice, He said over the bread, *this is my body*. He did not say this represents my body, this symbolizes my body, this is a token of my body, but *this is my body*. And notice that He also said, *given for you*. Given on the Cross. And then taking the chalice He said, drink all of you of this, for this is my blood of the New Covenant, shed for many to the remission of sins. Over the chalice of wine He said, *this is my blood*, not this represents, but *this is*.

Does our Lord mean what He says? We believe it. What makes our faith unique is this: that we do not pick and choose among the words of our Blessed Lord. We do not fool around with them. When He says *whose sins you forgive are forgiven them*, we believe it. That is why there is the Sacrament of Penance. And now when He says *this is my body, this is my blood*, we believe it.

So the law of communion continues through the universe. If the plants could speak, they would say to the animals: unless you eat me you shall not have life in you. If the animals could speak, they would say to man: unless you eat me you shall not have life in you. And Christ speaks to us and says: unless you eat me you shall not have life in you. The law of transformation holds sway. Chemicals are transformed into plants, plants into animals, animals into man, and man into Christ. Christ the Divine Pelican. According to the legend, the pelican wounds itself in order that it might nourish its young. So, He gave His life to sustain our life and the greatest joy in the world: His communion with the very life of God.

We are hungry for God. He is our most urgent need.

QUOTE: "I am not capable of doing big things, but I want to do everything, even the smallest things, for the greater glory of God." Saint Dominic Savio

POINT TO PONDER: Reflect on all the many ways human beings experience hunger. Use the four aspects of the human person as a starting point for your reflection—physical, emotional, intellectual, and spiritual.

VERSE TO LIVE: "Do not be anxious about anything, but in every situation, by prayer and petition, with thanksgiving, present your requests to God. And the peace of God, which transcends all understanding, will guard your hearts and your minds in Christ Jesus." Philippians 4:6-7

PRAYER: Lord Jesus, set a fire in my heart that is hungry to find the way, set a fire in my heart that is hungry to discover the truth, set a fire in my heart that is hungry for the fullness of life you spoke of when you walked the dusty roads of Galilee 2000 years ago. And remind me in all things that you are the Way, the Truth, and the Life. Amen.

FULTON SHEEN was an American bishop and pioneer in the use of technology to communicate the Gospel to the multitudes. He was the bestselling author of many books including *Finding True Happiness*, and during his lifetime was a beloved and world-renowned television personality, speaker, and retreat leader. This reflection was adapted from Fulton Sheen's talk, *Holy Eucharist as Sacrament.*

WANT TO GROW SPIRITUALLY?

Read *The Wisdom of Fulton Sheen*

by Fulton Sheen

and

Finding True Happiness

by Fulton Sheen

8. THE EUCHARIST: GOD'S HIDING & OUR SEEKING

— Bobby Angel —

Why are we kneeling before bread?

This is weird.

What am I supposed to do with my hands?

My knees hurt.

This is really weird . . . kneeling before a piece of bread . . .

I remember these thoughts swirling around my head when I was 17 years old, kneeling in a very small youth room during my first proper experience of Eucharistic Adoration. The priest placed the Communion wafer into this golden cross called a "Monstrance" (From the Latin word *mostrarae*, "to show") and all the other teens kneeled before it. I followed suit, unsure what was going on or what I was supposed to do.

This is really weird . . . kneeling before a piece of bread . . .

This is crazy . . .

Or . . . this is ***really*** *Jesus.*

I left that evening confused but somehow comforted. I wasn't sure of what questions to even start asking, but I felt a great peace that I never knew prior. It was the very "strangeness" of this encounter that drew me closer to Christ and sparked a desire to learn about my faith for the first time.

LIAR, LUNATIC, OR LORD

It dawned on me that either we truly were crazy as Catholics in worshiping, adoring, and consuming bread as "the Body of Christ," or it had to actually be the real thing. There could be no in-between. This is not a, "*This is true for you, but not for me*" situation. It either *isn't* Jesus (and we Catholics are idolatrous and dangerous), or it *really is*, and the Eucharist is truly the Bread of Life.

It's a situation akin to what C.S. Lewis called the "Trilemma": Jesus Christ was either a (1) liar, a (2) lunatic, or (3) Lord. We can't have Jesus as a "nice teacher" who also claims to be God in His ability to forgive sins, rise from the dead, and declare that you must eat His flesh to have eternal life (John 6:53-54). To be intellectually honest, we must take sides. He's either a dangerous or delusional man and we should flee Christianity—or He's telling the truth about Himself and He is indeed God Incarnate, the Word that became flesh to take away the sin of the world.

God had me on the hook and was slowly reeling me into His divine heart. It would take another year of coming back again and again to the youth group, asking questions with a deep desire to know (and not simply spit back answers for a test). The summer of 2003, I attended a Steubenville youth conference in Ohio. I can point to you the exact spot where I was kneeling on the floor of the fieldhouse venue on the Saturday night session of Adoration when my life forever changed. In that night of prayer and worship, I understood that Jesus knew me, loved me, and was waiting from all eternity for me to see Him in the beautiful simplicity of the Eucharist.

HIDE AND SEEK

But *why* would God hide from us?

If God loved us, wouldn't He "show up" and dispel

our difficulty in belief? And why, if the Eucharist is truly Christ, why hide within a simple wafer of bread?

Perhaps the most painful sentiment is that cry of the heart, “God, *where were you*?” This is not an inconsequential question. The problem of evil is real and many of us carry the wounds of neglect, abandonment, abuse, rejection, and pain. Maybe it was a major event or perhaps it was a slow trickle of our needs not being met. On this earth, we’re all the walking wounded. Back to the first question: *why* would God hide from us?

First of all, God’s ways are not our ways (Isaiah 55:8-9). God is God, and we are *not.* Only God has the divine perspective of the tapestry of all time and space. Before we start thinking that we’re entitled to understand the whole of reality, we have to first have a posture of humility—we don’t have all the answers and we never will on this side of eternity. What we participate in is not a problem to be solved but a great mystery to be experienced. God never said that we wouldn’t face suffering (or that He would take all our suffering away), but He did say He would be with us in the trials, wherever we go (Genesis 28:15).

And what more profound way could He be with us

than to make Himself into the *literal food* for our journey?

I think we'd be beyond overwhelmed with terror and awe, and have our faces melted off like in *Raiders of the Lost Ark*, if God "showed up" in the manner we often demand. God shields Himself constantly in Scripture (through clouds, angelic messengers, and the Burning Bush). Even after delivering Israel from bondage in Egypt and into the Promised Land, Moses was only allowed to see the "back" of God in passing, for no one could see God and live (Exodus 33:20).

Fast-forward to God revealing Himself through the Son as a carpenter of the backwater town of Nazareth and we see how God continues to humble Himself, first as a baby in Bethlehem (the City of Bread) and then to every age afterwards in the Eucharist (the Bread of Life). Our God is not one to reveal Himself in a bombastic, Hollywood-type manner. He speaks in the quiet, in the still small voice, and in unassuming bread.

A simple analogy here, but one that might prove poignant. Our kids love hide-and-seek. They want to play it over and over and over again. There's a delight in the simplicity of the game, of being sought after and being seen. To be hidden does not mean "absent" or that my child "disappeared." To be hidden doesn't mean God is playing games with us, but that He wants us to discover Him anew, with our own eyes.

To be hidden is the gleeful beckon of, "Come find me!"

PURSUE HIM

Kids are ever-patient with these ever-new games, even if we adults grow cynical and tired. Kids still delight in mysteries and so does God. Only the childlike can inherit the Kingdom of Heaven (Matthew 18:3). Only those with eyes to see could comprehend the childlike simplicity of appearing before us as humble bread.

The mystery, the delight of being found, and the desire to be pursued are, I believe, echoes of the heart of God within each of us to be both receiver and a seeker. The Church asserts, "God never ceases to draw man to Himself . . . He never ceases to call every man to seek Him, so as to find life and happiness." (CCC 27-30) Bring your questions and desires to Christ—"Seek and you will find; knock and it will be opened to you." (Matthew 7:7)

How beautiful is it then that God gives us the Eucharist? It is His eternal invitation to come find Him, the only one who can truly fulfill the deepest desires of our hearts. And so, whenever we yearn for meaning, feel tired and overwhelmed, become uncertain about the direction of our lives, or simply need to feel loved . . . we know just where to turn.

God awaits us always in the Eucharist. As long as we never tire of seeking Him there, we will find exactly what our souls need.

QUOTE: "All the darkness in the world cannot extinguish the light of a single candle." Saint Francis of Assisi

POINT TO PONDER: Are you chasing the wrong things?

VERSE TO LIVE: "Ask and you shall receive. Seek and you shall find. Knock and the door will be opened to you." Matthew 7:7

PRAYER: Lord, we spend our lives chasing things, people, and experiences. Help me to chase those that are worthy of me; those that are worthy of my hopes, dreams, faith and love; those that are worthy of my time—the precious time you have gifted me on this earth. Amen.

BOBBY ANGEL is a writer, speaker, and evangelist for the Catholic faith. He hosts the *Conversations* podcast. And, alongside his wife, he is the author of the book *Pray, Decide, and Don't Worry.*

WANT TO GROW SPIRITUALLY?

Read this novel,

Three Days:

The Search for the Boy Messiah

by Chris Stepien

9. THE ULTIMATE PROOF OF GOD'S LOVE

— Father Eric Boelscher —

How do we know that God loves us?

I'm sure you've been told many times by many good-intentioned people that "God loves you." But in a world full of broken people, messy relationships and an unfortunate amount of cruelty, it can feel like a trite or empty phrase.

Perhaps you'd like some more solid proof. That's understandable. Our culture has taught us to demand proof of everything, something solid, something sure, before we can ever confidently assent to anything.

And so, in this broken world, we're constantly looking for proof that the God of the universe is not just some uncaring, distant force but a deeply personal and loving God. We long for that to be true, but we have to ask ourselves, if that proof were given, would we actually accept it?

I think of St. Paul's first letter to the Corinthians where he says "For Jews demand signs and Greeks look for wisdom, but we proclaim Christ crucified, a stumbling block to Jews and foolishness to Gentiles, but to those who are called, Jews and Greeks alike, Christ the power of God and the wisdom of God. For the foolishness of God is wiser than human wisdom, and the weakness of God is stronger than human strength." (1 Cor 1:22-25)

With these words, St. Paul explains that if you are looking for proof that God's love is real, God has already given it. But He gives it in a way that is so counter to what we would ever imagine that it is difficult to accept. He gives it on the Cross.

The Cross is written up and down the pages of scripture, from the very first book to the last. Starting in the garden of Eden, we hear about the most sacred tree being the "tree of life." Even when Adam and Eve are expelled from the garden, it is with a hope that through the passion and sacrifice of a distant descendent, there might be some way back to this life-giving tree. Several chapters on, Abraham proves his faith to God by having his grown son carry wood up the mountain of Moriah (later known as one of the hills of Jerusalem) intending to sacrifice him as the Lord commanded, before God stays Abraham's hand. Before they go up the mountain, in Genesis 22:5, Abraham says that both he and his son will come back. This verse indicates that Abraham's faith assured him that whenever it comes to sacrifice, God will provide and always in mercy.

All throughout the remainder of the Old Testament, examples of God's mercy in sacrifice continue to appear. Prior to the Exodus, Moses and the Israelites are delivered by God's power and spared by his mercy during the sacrifice of Passover by marking the vertical and horizontal posts of their doors with blood. During the Exodus, when the Israelites are attacked by seraph serpents, they are saved yet again by God's mercy when He instructs them to look at the sign of sin mounted to a wooden pole and they will be spared. Perhaps most beautifully, in Psalm 22 King David describes what we will later know as the Lord's crucifixion, long before the Romans ever perfected this most barbaric practice. His psalm ends with beautiful lines of proven fidelity when he writes, "The generation to come will be told of the Lord, that they may proclaim to a people yet unborn the deliverance you have brought." In the books of the Prophets, specifically in the ninth chapter of Ezekiel, we hear that those who love real worship will receive God's mercy, and consequently be marked with a symbol upon their forehead that looks strikingly like a cross. With these excerpts, readers learn of the Cross and its gift of mercy through sacrifice in the Old Testament, well before the Gospels wherein Jesus instructs us repeatedly that we are to take up our own cross, just as He takes up His.

Beyond the Gospels, the New Testament continues to write of the Cross' gift of mercy through sacrifice. In fact, it can be found on almost every page of the New Testament. St. Paul spoke of it in the verses from Corinthians presented above. In chapters four and five of the Book of Revelation, St. John describes the worship of Heaven as resembling sacrifice. This sacrificial worship in Heaven all happens by God's will, and takes place right at the base of that promised tree of life.

Here's the real thing though, the thing that I think

you knew in your bones before you ever read a word of Scripture or any word in this book. Sacrifice is the language of love. There has not been a single meaningful relationship in human history that was not marked by some gift of sacrifice, one person to the other. Moreover, that's where mercy always comes from, and most of us learn this truth the hard way. When marriages need mending, families get fractured, or friends lose faith in each other, what is it that heals? It's sacrifice! It seems that the Cross is written on every page of our life, just as it is on every page of Scripture.

So, how can any of us be sure that God loves us? Perhaps this sounds foolish to some, and maybe too simple to others, but that proof can be found on every altar at every parish by every Catholic with the eyes to see it. Right in the middle of that worship, in that small white host raised to Heaven, there is a re-presentation of the one eternal sacrifice of Christ on His Cross. That is the very essence of the Eucharist. It is Christ himself, given up for you and me on the Cross, offered to us now and for eternity.

Whenever you see the Eucharist, you look upon the reality of Jesus' sacrifice on the Cross. The arms of that Cross stretch from the very beginning of time into eternity, they stretch from Heaven to earth, and let's not forget they stretch into every meaningful relationship any one of us will ever have.

An ancient order of monks and nuns called the Carthusians have a motto that says: "The Cross stands steady, as the world turns." I can't help but think that in our current world that struggles to believe in much of anything—where every one of us is searching for something solid, something sure, something of real substance—that Christ in His great mercy, has given us an immovable sign of His love. This sign is written in history, in your heart, and is given in every Eucharistic Sacrifice in every Catholic Church. Is that enough for you to know that God loves you? I honestly cannot imagine what more He could do to prove it.

QUOTE: "We do pray for mercy; And that same prayer doth teach us all to render the deeds of mercy." William Shakespeare

POINT TO PONDER: What area of your life do you need God and others to pour mercy into?

VERSE TO LIVE: "Therefore we do not lose heart. Though outwardly we are wasting away, yet inwardly we are being renewed day by day. For our light and momentary troubles are achieving for us an eternal glory that far outweighs them all. So we fix our eyes not on what is seen, but on what is unseen, since what is seen is temporary, but what is unseen is eternal." 2 Corinthians 4:16

PRAYER: Jesus, begin a revolution of love in my heart today. Teach me to love myself as you love me, so that I can love others who cross my path in a way that reminds them that you are the revolutionary the world needs in all places and at all times. Amen.

FATHER ERIC BOELSCHER is a priest in the Diocese of Covington, Kentucky, pastor to Saint Joseph parish and school community in Crescent Springs, Kentucky, and our beloved chaplain at Dynamic Catholic.

WANT TO GROW SPIRITUALLY?

Read

The Fourth Quarter of Your Life

by Matthew Kelly and Allen Hunt

10. THIRTY WORDS THAT REVOLUTIONIZED MY LIFE

— Allen Hunt —

The Lord Jesus, on the night he was betrayed, took bread, and when he had given thanks, he broke it and said, "This is my body, which is for you." These words revolutionized my life.

When I was in graduate school, I met Father Steven. Even though he was a Catholic priest and I was a Methodist pastor, we became lifelong friends. One day, Father Steven invited me to give a retreat to a group of cloistered Dominican nuns. After explaining that these women pray all day and never leave their monastery walls, I told him, "I've got to see this."

As soon as we got there, I knew something was different about the place. Sister Diane opened the door and my first thought was, "You may be the most attractive person I've ever met." She had this light emanating from her eyes, a radiance leaping off of her face. There was almost a glow about her. It was otherworldly. Holiness is attractive. It draws people to you.

Sister Diane led us back behind the cloister wall to the community room where all 50 nuns were gathered. When it came time for my talk, Father Steven introduced me and I got up in front of the nuns. I had to take a step back because, as I looked at their faces, I realized that almost all of them had that same radiance Sister Diane had. It took me a moment to get my composure back, but I managed to give my first talk. And then Father Steven gave his talk. And we did that for six straight Wednesdays.

On the last day of the retreat, a nun named Sister Rose got up and asked me a question:

"Allen, you're the first Methodist pastor that most of us have ever met. And I also want to tell you, after listening to you for these past six weeks, you sound really Catholic. So I have to ask you, why aren't you a part of the Church?"

I thought to myself, *That's a strange question. I am a part of the church. I mean, it says right here on my card: Allen,*

Pastor, United Methodist Church, C-H-U-R-C-H, church.

I told her, "I don't understand the question."

And she said, "Well, let me ask you again. Why aren't you a part of the Church?" Same question said the exact same way.

I said, "I guess what you're asking me is, why am I not Catholic?"

She said, "No. What I'm asking you is, why aren't you a part of the Church?" Same words. Gentle smile. Persistent, but gentle and loving. Three times in a row.

At this point all I could say was, "Sister Rose, I don't really understand your question, so I'm just going to tell you why I'm not Catholic. If I had to answer, I'd probably say that I'm not Catholic because I don't understand what you believe about Communion. For me, it's just obvious that the bread and the wine are symbols. They're special. They're important. They're holy. But to somehow believe that they're miraculously transformed into the body and blood of Jesus, literally, that just doesn't make sense to me."

I'll never forget Sister Rose's next response. She asked if I had my Bible and told me to open it to 1 Corinthians 11:23-26. So I did.

"These are the words from Saint Paul as he wrote to the church in Corinth" she said. Then she started to read: "For I received from the Lord what I also passed on to you: The Lord Jesus, on the night he was betrayed, took bread, and when he had given thanks, he broke it and said, 'This is my body, which is for you; do this in remembrance of me.'"

Sister Rose closed her Bible and she said, "Allen, what don't you understand?"

All the nuns and sisters giggled. We had a little bit of a laugh, and I wish I could say that at that moment the heavens opened and God called me into the Catholic Church. But that's not what happened. That encounter with Sister Rose was just the very first seed, planted in the back of my soul.

Over time, God led me home to the Catholic Church, but it was a long and difficult journey. The Eucharist was the central and greatest treasure that captivated my mind and heart. I began to experience an aching longing to receive Jesus—body, blood, soul, and divinity—in the Eucharist. I yearned to know Him in the most intimate of ways.

This led to a crisis of conscience for me as a Methodist pastor, until I could no longer maintain my position. I stepped aside from leading 15,000 people each week because I could no longer deny the genius of the Catholic Church and the absolute beauty of the Real Presence of Jesus in the Eucharist. And on January 6th, 2008, I entered the Catholic Church and received the Eucharist for the first time. I've never looked back.

I love so many things about being Catholic, but what I love most is the privilege and joy of receiving Jesus in the Eucharist. But I also know how easy it is to take things for granted. We do that a lot in life, and as Catholics, we do that a lot with the extraordinary faith we have been gifted.

So here is my challenge for you and me. Let us never take for granted the extraordinary treasure of the Eucharist. Let us never become numb to the fact that Jesus wants to give Himself fully to you and me at every Mass. He really is there, waiting to transform our lives. That is the greatest treasure we could ever hope to have.

QUOTE: "Pray to be ever ready for God's will even when it takes you by surprise." Saint Mary MacKillop

POINT TO PONDER: There is one thing that God is trying to say to you at the moment. You are resisting it, avoiding it, ignoring it. Surrender to it, and your life will change beginning today.

VERSE TO LIVE: "Therefore, if anyone is in Christ, he is a new creation. The old has passed away; behold, the new has come." 2 Corinthians 5:17

PRAYER: Lord, fill me with your light and never let me forget that there is nothing more attractive than holiness. Amen.

ALLEN HUNT is the author of a number of bestselling books, including *No Regrets* and *Confessions of a Mega Church Pastor*. While serving as an evangelical mega church pastor, Allen began a remarkable journey culminating in his conversion to Catholicism. He now helps lead Dynamic Catholic in the mission to help people rediscover the genius and relevance of Catholicism.

WANT TO GROW SPIRITUALLY?

Read

Messy & Foolish:

How to Make a Mess, Be a Fool, and Evangelize the World

by Matt Warner

11. WHY I LIED TO MY PASTOR ABOUT FIRST COMMUNION

— Sister Helena Burns, FSP —

I made my First Communion at seven years old, pretending to believe in the Real Presence of Jesus Christ. Good Father Hurley went to great pains to make sure we second-graders understood that the small white wafer was not ordinary bread. He explained that once he said the words of consecration, it would become the body, blood, soul and divinity of the Lord Jesus Christ. He told us that Jesus remained in the Eucharist when He was placed in the tabernacle. He had us practice consuming an unconsecrated host without chewing it. He even interviewed each of us at our homes with our parents present to make sure we had faith. So, I lied.

Why did I lie? I wanted the First Communion party,

the pretty white dress, the presents—to just go along doing what all my peers were doing, of course. Why didn't I believe? Because it sounded ridiculous to me that God (who I did kind of believe in) would become bread to be eaten by humans. I was never a terribly literal child (I was always seeking deeper meanings), so I never pictured Jesus with tiny dollhouse furniture inside the tabernacle like many children do. Thanks be to God, the adults in my parish weren't pushing the bogus notion of "it's just a symbol," or "it's just a commemoration of the Last Supper." I got what the adults were trying to communicate to us: the Mass is the real deal. I just wasn't buying it.

As I grew up (going to public schools and CCD), the little faith I had turned into the faith of the Deists. I believed in God the Creator, a watchmaker God who wound up the world and then stepped back, stepped away from His Creation and was no longer involved in it. The God of the Deists is not a personal God, is not a caring God. The God of the Deists is not the Most Holy Trinity. He doesn't listen to or answer prayers, so we're basically alone in the universe. The one thing I believed the Creator expected us to do was figure everything out by ourselves, with each individual bearing a tremendous moral responsibility to get it right and live right. (I was also quite an existentialist.)

By fifteen, I was quietly suicidal. It wasn't a chemical imbalance, or even sad or bad circumstances in my life. In fact, I had it pretty darn good. Everything was percolating nicely, except . . . I didn't know why I was alive. I didn't only want to know why I in particular was alive, I needed to know what the purpose of human life was in general: the subjective and the objective. I asked my friends what the purpose of life was. Most of them responded: "Why ask why?" I asked my mother, who gave the definitive, comprehensive *Baltimore Catechism* answer: "God made me to know Him, to love Him, and to serve Him in this world and to be happy with Him forever in the next" (which made great sense to me later), but the problem was, my God was different than this personal God.

This is where my story goes beyond what I understand. I'm fully aware what happened next does not happen for most people. In fact, I'm still working to unpack just what it was that happened to me and the mysterious way God was working in my life.

One night, at my wit's end, I had the idea that my Deist Creator God just might be able to hear me and help me. I knelt by my bed and prayed: "O God, if You can hear me, I need Your help because I don't know why I'm alive and I don't want to live anymore." I went to sleep. It would be the last night I would have to live with the sense of being enveloped in a cold, dark void.

The next morning, when I awoke, everything changed. I could feel God's presence. (I now believe this was God the Father.) I knew He loved me. I knew many things, and had many of my questions answered (something I later found out is called "infused knowledge"). I knew that it didn't really matter exactly what I accomplished in life. What mattered was that God was waiting for me in Heaven, and He was more excited than I was about my going to Heaven to be with Him forever. My next query was wondering if Jesus really was God or not. I looked at the crucifix on my wall that had been there since I was born, and remembered how much I loved doing the Stations of the Cross during Lent as a child. At that moment I was given the grace to believe that Jesus was God.

But there were so many Christian denominations.

Which one was real? I determined to start investigating by visiting all my Christian friends' different churches. But wait. Why not start with the Catholic Church? OK. What makes the Catholic Church different from all the other Christian churches? The Most Blessed Sacrament. It wasn't like each Christian church was claiming: "No! He's in our box! We have Him!" They didn't even have boxes. Soooo . . . if Jesus was truly present in the tabernacles of Catholic churches all over the world, then this was His Church, and I needed to stop disbelieving and fighting against many of her other doctrines.

But how would I know if Jesus was in the Eucharist, as Father Hurley had earnestly, unsmilingly tried to make sure we understood? If I asked Catholics or read a Catholic book, they'd say "yes." If I asked other Christians or read a Christian book, they'd say "no." I finally decided that if God had spoken to me once, He could do it again. But rather than just unceremoniously ask Him on the spot, I chose a day to solemnize the question. This was a big deal. On the given day, I went to my parish church, Our Lady of Mercy, and said these exact words: "Jesus, if you are in the tabernacle, I will accept the Catholic Church's teachings, lock, stock, and barrel, stop rejecting them, and strive to understand them. So, are you there, Lord?" I looked intently at the white and gold repository and instantly heard: "Yes, I am here," and He was nodding but I didn't see His head or His face, and I have no idea how that works, but all I can tell you is that He was emphatic. I just as instantly believed. Well, alrighty then. I had some work to do. (At this point in my life, I had also become a rabid radical feminist who despised the Catholic Church.)

Four days later, God called me to be a Sister. No moss grows under our Savior's sandals. As I researched various congregations, I knew that I wanted one that prized Eucharistic Adoration as part of their spirituality. I found what I was looking for in the Daughters of St. Paul.

God could have communicated with me before I asked, but I believe He waited until I prayed wholeheartedly to show me the importance of prayer. God could have infused the knowledge that He was present in the Eucharist, but I believe He wanted me to encounter His Presence up close and personal.

Looking back, I am still amazed at the extraordinary grace God poured into my life right when I felt like everything was hopeless. I don't think I'll ever be able to make sense of it all. But that's ok. God invites us to know Him in mysterious ways. What matters isn't that we grasp why. What matters is whether or not we say "yes." There's no more powerful way to do that than to turn to him in the Eucharist.

QUOTE: "Lay all your cares about the future trustingly in God's hands, and let yourself be guided by the Lord just like a little child." Saint Edith Stein

POINT TO PONDER: Next time you think that God has stopped speaking to you, consider the alternative reality that perhaps you have stopped listening to His voice in your life.

VERSE TO LIVE: "We know that all things work together for good for those who love God who are called according to his purpose." Romans 8:28

PRAYER: Jesus, teach me to value your way of doing things above all other ways.

SISTER HELENA BURNS, FSP is a member of the Daughters of St. Paul, an international congregation founded to communicate God's Word through the media. In addition, she is a speaker, filmmaker, and writer for *The Catholic Register.*

WANT TO GROW SPIRITUALLY?

Read

Catholic and Christian:

An Explanation of Commonly Misunderstood Catholic Beliefs

by Alan Schreck

and

Rediscover the Rosary

by Matthew Kelly

12. WHY DIDN'T ANYONE TELL ME THIS?

— Matt Warner —

The loud party music and laughing from the booze cruise passing just offshore was an odd backdrop for what broke my brain on the sandy beach in the Bahamas that day. Lying in the sun, book in hand, I turned to my buddy in absolute astonishment, "Did you know about all this?!" I held up the half-finished Catholic apologetics book I'd recently been given—the first I'd ever read.

I grew up Catholic, never questioning our beliefs. Catholics believed it. I was Catholic. So I believed it. That was enough. But this . . . this was too much. I was now faced with the realization that my religion was not just a personal preference, or a beautiful way of life passed on by my family, but that it also all happened to be true.

"Two, or three, to one!" said the Bahamian beach peddler, interrupting my epiphany in the sand. *Two or three to one*, I soon discovered, was the ratio of women to men on the booze cruise he was selling tickets for, an appealing pitch to the many young men yearning for more by the sea that day. But I had been hooked by something more—the Truth. And it was already dragging me into deeper waters than any booze cruise could go.

That moment on the beach cascaded into many more just like it. On issue after issue of Catholic teaching—some of them shocking and strange—I discovered deeply satisfying reasons for everything. Believing everything the Church taught all of a sudden felt so straightforward and logical (though certainly not always easy), even for something as outlandish as the Eucharist.

Believing that Jesus' body and blood is truly present in the Eucharist seems silly on the surface, but it kept making more and more sense from every angle I looked at it:

- Scripture is clear on it. [1]
- The first generation of Christians believed it. [2]
- The early Christians died for it. [3]
- As Peter Kreeft sums up well, "Until Zwingli (in the 1500s), no orthodox, traditional, non-hereti-

> cal, mainline, historic, apostolic Christian ever believed . . . the Eucharist is only a holy symbol of Christ, not Christ Himself."[4]

The list of reasons just kept going on. It became clear that the only logical worldview as a Christian is a Eucharistic one. Learning this made me eager to share these same revelations with everyone around me. Surely everyone just needed the same apologetics book and they would believe too. Unfortunately, I soon found it was not that simple.

Since that moment, I've spent my entire adult life figuring out how to help the Church better communicate her message successfully. What are the best mediums and methods to use? Why do our efforts sometimes work so well, and other times fail so miserably? How can two people see the same thing so differently? How do we share the Good News in a culture that thinks it's old news? It's a complicated and multifaceted challenge, and an ongoing journey. But one thing I've learned for sure is that no matter the soundness of the apologetics or the truth-bombs dropped, the effectiveness of any message is always limited by a person's capacity to receive it. Successful communication (and therefore evangelization) often requires first increasing a person's capacity to receive the message before the reasonable argument or words you say have much impact.

That capacity for a person to receive a message is determined by many things, such as their relationship with the person speaking, their perception of (in this case) the Church, their own immediate needs, experiences of suffering, and many other factors that are independent of the words we say or the finely-reasoned arguments we share. More than all that still, and perhaps the biggest factor influencing one's capacity to receive a given message, is their *worldview*. What kind of story do they think they're in?

The Modern Story leaves no room for the supernatural. It tells of a round Earth, but a flat universe—squashed down to only include the particles and forces the natural sciences can detect and measure. That worldview not only excludes much of reality, it misses the most important parts. And it certainly leaves no room for the Eucharist. We have a crisis of imagination.

I used to think my imagination was for seeing things that aren't real. In truth, it's for seeing things that are the most real—because the most important parts of life are invisible. You need an imagination to account for all the real things that can't be seen, like thoughts. Or heavy things that can't be weighed, like values. Movements of the most powerful creatures, like angels. Sacrifices that can't be measured, like love. Actions that are most important, like prayer. Forces that hold this universe together, like grace. Miracles hidden beneath the ordinary, like the Eucharist. Reality includes all of those things, but it takes a well-formed imagination to see them. To imagine them is not to invent them in your mind, but to put into your mind what is really out there and include them as part of the story you're in.

As Antoine de Saint-Exupéry said, "If you want to build a ship, don't drum up the men to gather wood, divide the work, and give orders. Instead, teach them to yearn for the vast and endless sea." If you teach them to yearn for the vast and endless sea, they will naturally build the ship anyway. Furthermore, until they have such a yearning, you're wasting your breath trying to get them to care about how the ship works or why it's needed. When somebody is content to continue booze-cruising the shallows or sitting on the shore, a ship that takes them over the horizon (the Church) will remain quite irrelevant.

The modern imagination needs an expansion before it can understand the explanation. One must first understand the incredible story we are all already in—God's story, the story of salvation history. That's where one discovers that the secret to happiness and the purpose of this life is not to enjoy the beaches and the trivialities of the shallows, but to leave them behind and set sail for what lies beyond.

Don't forget, we live in a world where men rise from the dead, where death is only the beginning, where Someone put you on that beach for a reason and gave you a meaningful mission to go on a grand adventure. When you live in a world like that—a supernatural world—it becomes not only logical, but rather natural to take Jesus at His word when He says (in John 6:55) that "my flesh is true food, and my blood is true drink."

QUOTE: "Reason is in fact the path to faith, and faith takes over when reason can say no more." Thomas Merton

POINT TO PONDER: Do you sense that God is calling you to step away from the comfort that defines your life and participate in life more meaningfully?

VERSE TO LIVE: "And when he had ceased speaking, he said to Simon, 'Put out into the deep waters and let down your nets for a catch.'" Luke 5:4

PRAYER: Jesus, give me the courage to follow your call, the insight to foresee the regrets I will have if I don't, and the boldness to invite others to do the same. Amen.

MATT WARNER is the author of *Messy & Foolish: How to Make a Mess, Be a Fool, and Evangelize the World.* He is also the founder of Flocknote, the premier communication management tool helping Catholic parishes engage, inform, and inspire their parishioners.

WANT TO GROW SPIRITUALLY?

Read
The Turning Point:
Eight Encounters with Jesus that Will Change Your Life
by Allen Hunt
and
Everybody Evangelizes About Something
by Matthew Kelly

1. John 6, 1 Cor 11, and so many others.

2. The first generations of Christians, by their writings (Didache 60-100 AD, St. Ignatius of Antioch 110 AD, St. Justin Martyr 150 AD, and others), clearly believed in the Real Presence. And the idea that the people who lived with and learned directly from the disciples somehow got this central teaching so incredibly wrong (and without real protest from other Christians) is inconceivable.

3. St. Tarcisius (and others) clearly died with a belief in the Real Presence. He wouldn't have risked his life to sneak a symbolic piece of bread to imprisoned Christians. He gave his life because it was more than just a symbol and central to the life and salvation of every Christian.

4. Peter Kreeft, Jesus Shock.

CONCLUSION: GET CLOSE AND STAY CLOSE

— Matthew Kelly —

What's the most beautiful church you have ever been in? How did it make you feel?

I began speaking and writing when I was nineteen. At the time I was in business school, and since then, I have been blessed to travel in more than fifty countries. Few things inspire me more than traveling. There is something about experiencing different people, places and cultures that opens our hearts and minds.

I grew up Catholic and my experience of the Catholic Church was mostly limited to our parish, St. Martha's in suburban Sydney. But through travel I began to see how vast and impressive the Catholic Church is, in so many ways.

One thing that becomes abundantly clear when you start traveling is that the world is full of beautiful Catholic churches. Have you ever wondered why we build such beautiful churches? I can tell you this: It's not about the art or the architecture. It's because we believe that Jesus is truly present in the Eucharist.

Stand in St. Peter's Basilica in Rome, Notre Dame or Sacre Coeur in Paris, St. Mary's Cathedral in Sydney, Duomo Cathedral in Milan, Las Lajas Sanctuary in Columbia, St. Patrick's Cathedral in New York, the Basilica of the National Shrine of the Immaculate Conception in Washington DC, or any of a thousand other incredible Catholic churches around the world and you will feel awe and a sense of the sacred.

What do these beautiful churches really say to us? They say that there is something greater here than art or architecture, something more than history—and not just some*thing* . . . but some*one*. That someone is Jesus Christ, truly present in the Eucharist, present in all these churches, and present in the tabernacle in your local church.

That's why I love stopping by a church for a few quiet minutes.

We all have questions that we need answered, and we all need advice from time to time. But when we need advice we tend to ask people who know just about nothing about nothing, instead of going to the man who has all the answers.

All the answers are in the tabernacle. Jesus has all the answers and he patiently waits for us in the tabernacle, day and night, to share those answers with us. Next time you are grappling with a decision, stop by your church and ask Jesus for his advice. Receiving Jesus in the Eucharist is the ultimate spiritual experience, but there is also something powerful about just sitting in his presence.

In the Gospels we read time and time again about Jesus leaving his disciples and the crowds and going to a place set apart. In the first chapter of Mark's gospel we read, "In the morning, while it was still very dark, he got up and went out to a deserted place, and there he prayed." (Mark 1:35) If Jesus needed this time in silence and solitude, how much more do you think we need it? The world is a busy and noisy place, and all of that tends to distract us from what matters most.

It is getting harder and harder to find a quiet place in

this world, but one of the great gifts the Catholic Church gives to us all is places that are set apart for quiet reflection. Churches and chapels, retreat centers and monasteries—over the centuries the Church has established places in almost every community on earth for us to be still and quiet and reflect on what is happening within us and around us.

Once again, I want to encourage you to establish the habit of daily prayer in your life. This is a foundational habit that will serve you well for the rest of your life. The sooner you start taking your spiritual life seriously, the happier you will be.

Get close to God and stay close to God.

Years ago, I received a letter from a priest who had worked as a lay missionary in China before he returned to his homeland of America and became a priest. He shared many stories about the Church in China, but there is one that made a huge impression on me. It is a story I have told hundreds of times and one that always humbles me.

Many years after being ordained a priest, he returned to China, incognito, for a brief visit. Even today, there are priests and bishops in prison in China for nothing other than refusing to let the Communist government control their churches. For this reason, nobody in China knew that he was a priest.

On the second night of his visit, he was awakened in the middle of the night by the noise of people moving around the house. A little scared, he got up and went to his door. Opening it, he asked one of the men living in the house what was going on.

His Chinese host replied, "We're going to the wall."

He inquired further, "What is the wall?"

His host replied, "Come with us and we will show you."

There were more than twenty people living in the small house, and while none of them knew he was a priest, they knew he could be trusted.

Not satisfied with the answers he had received, he went downstairs and found one of the older women whom he had known many, many years earlier and asked her, "What's going on? Where are you all going?"

She gently replied, "We're going to the wall."

He persisted, "Yes, but what is the wall?"

She replied with the same gentleness, "Come with us and we will show you."

He got dressed and ventured out into the night with the group. They walked for miles and along the way other groups joined them. Now, all together, they numbered almost 120 men, women and children. Soon they came to a forest and as they began to walk into it, he noticed that some of the men in the group were climbing trees.

Several minutes later they came to a clearing in the forest, and in the middle of the clearing was a small wall about four feet tall, from an old, derelict building. The old woman turned to him and smiled with all the love in her heart, and though he sensed an incredible excitement in her, he did not know what to make of it. The people seemed excited, but he was scared.

Looking up into the trees, he noticed that there was a circle of men in the trees surrounding the clearing, and now, as the group came close to the wall, they fell down on their knees before it.

Moments later, one man got up and walked toward the wall, then, reaching out with one hand, he took a single brick out of the wall. Behind the brick was a tiny monstrance holding the Eucharist. The group spent one hour in silent prayer before the Blessed Sacrament, and then the same man got up, approached the wall, and replaced the single brick. The men came down from their lookout positions in the trees and the group went quietly home.

The next day he told the people that he was a priest and they told him that they had not had Mass in their village for ten years. Once or twice a week they would go to the wall in the middle of the night, risking their lives, to spend an hour with Jesus, truly present in the Eucharist.

The following night, the priest said Mass at the wall and replaced the host. It was one of the highlights of his priesthood.

I am not sure we appreciate the power of God present among us in every tabernacle in every church. If this priest had been discovered that night, he would have been imprisoned and tortured, and the rest of the group would have been imprisoned and quite possibly executed. They knew this all too well, and it was a risk they were willing to take.

Now, most of us do not find ourselves in such extraordinary circumstances. But we do all have questions in our hearts and challenges in our lives. We are all seeking clarity, healing, peace, and purpose.

Experience has taught me time and time again that all the answers are in that tabernacle. I can go to many people in my life and ask them what they think I should do in a given situation, but nothing compares to sitting before Jesus in the tabernacle and placing my question before him.

So here is my invitation to you: Stop by a church for ten minutes each day this week and spend time in the quiet. Sit before Jesus in the tabernacle. If you can, do it first thing in the morning. You will find that your days are more fruitful and focused, and filled with a passion that is invigorating and a joy that is intoxicating.

Jesus awaits you in the Eucharist. Come into the silence and let Him change your life.

NOTES

NOTES

NOTES

NOTES

NOTES

NOTES

NOTES

NOTES

NOTES

NOTES

NOTES

NOTES